Cambridge English Readers

Level 3

Series editor: Philip Prowse

The House by the Sea

Patricia Aspinall

W0215441

CAMBRIDGE
UNIVERSITY PRESS

CAMBRIDGE UNIVERSITY PRESS
Cambridge, New York, Melbourne, Madrid, Cape Town, Singapore, São Paulo, Delhi

Cambridge University Press
The Edinburgh Building, Cambridge CB2 8RU, UK

www.cambridge.org
Information on this title: www.cambridge.org/9780521775786

© Cambridge University Press 1999

This publication is in copyright. Subject to statutory exception
and to the provisions of relevant collective licensing agreements,
no reproduction of any part may take place without the written
permission of Cambridge University Press.

First published 1999
15th printing 2009

Printed in Italy by L.E.G.O. S.p.A.

A catalogue record for this publication is available from the British Library

ISBN 978-0-521-77578-6 paperback
ISBN 978-0-521-68658-7 paperback plus audio CD pack

Cambridge University Press has no responsibility for the persistence or
accuracy of URLs for external or third-party Internet websites referred to in
this publication, and does not guarantee that any content on such websites is,
or will remain, accurate or appropriate. Information regarding prices, travel
timetables and other factual information given in this work are correct at
the time of first printing but Cambridge University Press does not guarantee
the accuracy of such information thereafter.

Contents

Chapter 1	Old friends	6
Chapter 2	Waiting for Linda	12
Chapter 3	Mad Tom	19
Chapter 4	A voice in the dark	24
Chapter 5	The smell of death	30
Chapter 6	Dead father	35
Chapter 7	She still loves me	42
Chapter 8	Too many questions	48
Chapter 9	Whose fault is it?	54
Chapter 10	The yellow dress	60

Characters

Carl Anderson: a businessman. He lives and works in London.
Linda Anderson: Carl's wife. She buys the house by the sea.
Mary Banks: the owner of the Ancient Mariner pub in Little Moreton.
Police Constable (PC) Grant: the young policeman in Great Moreton.
Melissa: a friend of Linda's.
John: a journalist and old friend of Carl's – they went to university together.
Tom Parker: he lives in a car on the beach in Little Moreton.
Bill Parker: Tom's brother and a taxi driver in Little Moreton.

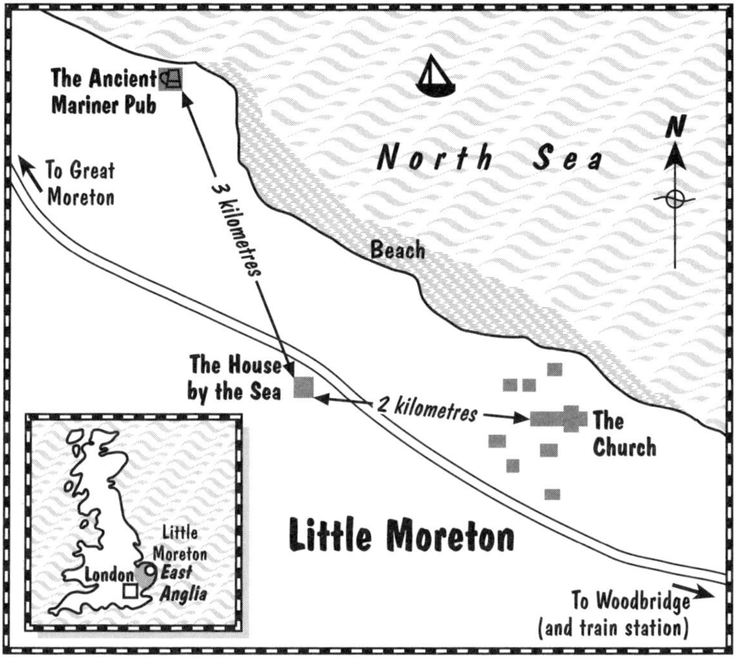

The Ancient Mariner Pub
North Sea
N
To Great Moreton
3 kilometres
Beach
The House by the Sea
2 kilometres
The Church
Little Moreton
Little Moreton
East Anglia
London
To Woodbridge (and train station)

Chapter 1 *Old friends*

It was lunchtime. I'd been in the *Jolly Sailor* pub in west London for about half an hour, when I saw a man sitting by himself in a corner of the room. Although I didn't know his name I was sure I knew him from somewhere. He had grey hair and he was looking out of the window at the River Thames.

I don't usually go to the pub at lunchtime, but it was the birthday of one of the other journalists at work. There were four of us. I asked them if they knew the man sitting in the corner. They looked over, but no-one knew him. I don't know why, but I just kept looking at him, trying to remember.

Finally, when we were all about to go back to work, the man turned round and looked straight at me. He knew me, I could see, because he smiled at me. Who was he? Then I realised it was someone I had been at university with five years ago. I couldn't remember his name immediately. He looked so old. He started to get up from his chair and I walked over to him. As I got closer I remembered his name.

'Carl,' I said, 'good to see you. What are you doing here?' I held out my hand.

'John, what a surprise! It's been such a long time.' He shook my hand and then put both hands on my arms. 'It's good to see you. You know, you're the first person I've seen from university for a long time. Those were good times, weren't they?'

It was clear that Carl was pleased to see me, but at first he wasn't sure what to say to me. He looked so different from the young, happy student I used to know. We were the same age but he looked a lot older than me. His hair was going grey and his face had a worried look. He was also much thinner than I remembered him.

Carl pointed at the seat he had just left. 'Let's sit down,' he said. 'I'll get you a drink.' I had to go back to work, but Carl was an old friend, a good friend – we'd had a lot of fun together at university. I couldn't say no.

'Yes,' I said, 'OK.' I told my friends from work that I would come back to the office soon. They left and I waited while Carl bought two drinks. It was hard to believe this was the same man I had been to university with. He looked so white and thin. Had something happened to him? Maybe he's just been in hospital, I thought.

Because I'm a journalist I always ask questions, but when Carl came back with the drinks, I didn't say anything about the way he looked.

'So, Carl,' I said, 'I've just been trying to remember the last time we met. I think it was at your wedding. That was quite a day, wasn't it?' Carl just nodded his head and smiled in a sad way. I didn't know what else to say, so I kept talking.

'Isn't it terrible that we haven't seen each other since then?' I said. 'How's Linda? Have you got any kids yet?' Carl stopped smiling and looked at me strangely. I knew I'd said the wrong thing, but I had to ask about his wife Linda. Linda went to the same university as us and she was beautiful. We were all good friends and we'd had a lot of fun together at university. Linda was fun to be with.

Carl had always been a serious person. He'd worked very hard and did well in his exams. When I used to try and make him go out for the evening he often said that he had too much work to do. I thought that Linda would soon get tired of him. Sometimes Linda and I went out together to have fun and left Carl with his books.

She must have liked the fact that he was serious because a year after they had finished at university Carl and Linda got married. It was a great wedding and they both looked so happy. They were obviously very much in love.

Had something happened to their marriage? Something must have happened to them since then, but I was afraid to ask.

Carl now looked at me in a serious way. I could see he wasn't happy. He was wearing a suit, but he wasn't wearing a tie and I wanted to ask him if he was working at the moment. But I didn't ask him and, as we drank our beer, I told him about what I'd been doing for the last four or five years. I told him how I'd found it difficult to get a job when I first left university.

'You know, Carl, I was never able to study like you did, and when I had to go and get a job I found it really hard. For a couple of years I worked on small newspapers all over the place. I spent two years in Devon. Beautiful but very quiet . . .'

I thought that Carl might want to know how I moved to a big national newspaper, how hard I now worked, but I could see he wasn't very interested. He kept looking out of the window at the river.

'. . . So finally, about six months ago, I decided it was time to come to London. There was nothing to keep me in Devon. No family, you know? I haven't been able to find a girl who wants to marry me yet. Perhaps I never will!' I said. For the first time since I had started telling him about myself Carl seemed to be listening.

'Don't work too hard if you do get married . . .' Carl said. 'I worked too hard and it finished my marriage.'

'Oh dear,' I replied. 'What happened, Carl? You don't look very happy. Where's Linda?'

'Happy? You're right, John. No, I'm not happy and I'm not sure I ever will be again . . .' He stopped talking and looked out of the window again. He finished his beer and then said, 'But you don't want to hear my story . . .'

But I *did* want to hear his story. After all, I was a journalist. I wrote stories as a job. I was always interested in stories. And I was especially interested in Carl's story. He was my friend. So was Linda. Of course I wanted to know.

'Tell me what happened with you and Linda,' I said. He looked at me for a minute to see if I was serious and then said, 'You know, when Linda agreed to marry me I thought I had everything. It was wonderful. I got a good job in London as soon as we left university. It was hard work – I was working most weekends – and for a couple of years we didn't take a holiday. But it was good money and we soon had enough to buy a flat. Linda had her friends and she seemed to like her job as well. We liked doing the same things, I thought, and I hoped that I'd soon have more time for us to spend together . . .' He stopped talking for a few seconds.

'It was Linda's idea to buy the house by the sea. It was going to be a place we could go to together at weekends. She loved the place. I understand why now,' he said, and then laughed in a sad way.

'Linda said London was dirty and noisy and the flat was boring. You know Linda, John. If she didn't like something she always said it was boring.'

He stopped for a moment and then in a voice full of anger he said: 'I wish I'd never seen that house. Never mind, John. You don't want to hear all this.'

I felt uncomfortable. This was not the Carl I used to know. I looked at my watch. It was nearly two o'clock. I had to go back to work, but I also wanted to know what had happened to my old friend, what had changed him so much.

'I'm sorry, Carl, I'd really like to hear your story, but I have to get back to work. Look, why don't we meet somewhere another night?'

We decided to meet in a pub we both knew the next evening. It was close to where I lived and was a much quieter place than the *Jolly Sailor*. I thought it would be easier for Carl to tell his story.

I was a bit late leaving work the next day and when I got to the pub Carl was already there. He was sitting with his back to the door in a quiet corner. I walked over to him and he stood up quickly. He looked worried.

'I'm pleased you're here,' he said. 'I thought perhaps you weren't coming.'

'Of course I came,' I said. 'Sit down and I'll get the beers.' When I returned with two beers, Carl said:

'Thanks for coming. I've been thinking, and I really feel

I need to tell someone about what happened. Since I saw you yesterday, I haven't been able to do anything. I couldn't sleep last night.'

I could see that Carl looked tired.

'And because you know Linda, and you're a friend . . .' said Carl.

'Well, Carl,' I said. 'Please tell me about it. I don't like to see you looking so unhappy. What happened to Linda? What happened between you?'

Chapter 2 *Waiting for Linda*

Carl looked into my eyes and began his story. This is what he told me:

Three years ago Linda decided she wanted to have a holiday house by the sea. She said we could go for weekends when we wanted. I thought it was a good idea to get away from our busy lives in London. Linda started to look for something and after a few months she found this house in East Anglia, in a village called Little Moreton. You won't have heard of it. It's just a few houses by the beach, a pub and a church. That's all . . .

I shall never forget the day we got married. Linda looked beautiful and we were so happy. We thought we had everything! Linda was working for a small company in the south east of London and my job was going well. I had to work long hours and sometimes at the weekends. But it was well-paid and it was interesting work. Linda didn't seem to mind and anyway she had lots of friends – the flat was always full of Linda's friends. In fact, sometimes I had to say to her: 'Come on, Linda, let's just have a quiet night tonight.' 'You're so boring, Carl,' she used to say.

You remember what fun she was, don't you John? She loved being with people. But with my job I had to get to bed early – I was up at six in the morning and on the way to work by seven.

Anyway, we had a good life. We were never short of

money and Linda could buy whatever she wanted. For a couple of years we didn't go on holiday . . .

So Linda bought this house and started to go down every weekend to get the place ready, to make it look nice and pretty. I went there when I could, but I was getting busier and busier at work – they were giving me more and more to do, and it was very difficult to say no!

And with a flat in London and a house by the sea we needed the money as well. Sometimes she went to the house with one of her friends. When she came back she always looked healthy and happy. It was good for her and it was good for me because I could continue with my work. Or I thought it was good for me . . .

Anyway, when the house was completely ready, Linda wanted me to go down and see how pretty it was looking. Unfortunately, there was an important meeting in Paris which I had to go to. For the next few weeks Linda was angry with me.

Then, one evening, she didn't come home from work. She phoned me to say she was staying with her friend, Melissa. 'Melissa and I are going to the cinema and you're always working late . . .'

It was true. I often came home late from work, and brought work home, too. There wasn't enough time in the day to do everything. Linda didn't understand how difficult it was for me at work.

But I didn't understand how unhappy Linda was. She didn't come home for the next three nights. She phoned each day to say she and Melissa were doing something different. I was angry, but what could I do? I wanted her to come back so much.

I decided I had to do something. I had to change. I had to stop working so much and spend more time with Linda.

On the Friday morning I phoned Linda at Melissa's house. It was Melissa who answered.

'Hi there, Carl. You want to speak to Linda?' Melissa said.

'Yes please, Melissa.'

'You know you should spend more time with your wife. You always put your job first.' I hadn't expected this from Melissa. I didn't reply. Then she gave the phone to Linda.

'What is it, Carl? I'm in a hurry. I'm late for work already.' Her voice sounded flat. I was thinking quickly. What could I say that would make her want to come home?

'Darling, we have to talk. I'm sorry about not seeing much of you. I promise I'm going to change. Look, what about this weekend? Let's go to the house by the sea together.' I hoped so much she would say yes. She didn't say anything for a minute.

'OK Carl. If you want to go there, that's fine.' I was so happy she had agreed. But then she said, 'I'm going to the office party this evening. I'll meet you at the house.'

I wasn't very happy that she couldn't come with me immediately. I wanted to tell her on the drive how much I loved her and show her how sorry I was. I didn't know then it was already too late, that it was already over.

'OK, Linda. That's fine. Will you come down on the train? I'll meet you at the station. You could ring me at the pub.' We didn't have a phone at the house.

'Fine. OK. See you then,' she said. We agreed that she would ring the pub and tell me which train she was taking.

For the first time in months I left work early and drove to Little Moreton. On the way I stopped and bought a bottle of champagne. Linda loved champagne. I prefer a good glass of beer, myself, but this was going to be Linda's weekend.

I arrived at the house in the afternoon. It was late October and starting to get dark. I parked at the side of the house. The ground around the house was wet and I saw that another car had been there. I didn't like the idea of someone else using my private parking place.

I unlocked the door and went in. I put my bag upstairs in the bedroom and saw that Linda had left clothes and shoes behind. It was like a real home to her, I thought. I went down to the kitchen and looked out of the window. From there I could see the sea. It was grey, not the blue sea of summer, and the sky was a dirty white colour.

But we would still enjoy a walk by the sea. I went to put the champagne in the fridge. I saw Linda had forgotten to empty it before she left. That was three weeks ago. There was cheese and eggs and a few other things. I took out two bottles of milk and started to pour them down the sink. I thought they would smell horrible, but they didn't. That was a little strange, but I thought that Linda must have come down one day and left them there.

So I made myself a cup of tea and went and sat on the sofa. The house was the same as before. No phone or television. I liked that. I preferred to be quiet when we weren't in London. I looked at my watch. It was half past five. Linda was probably on her way to the office party, I thought.

I picked up a newspaper which had been left on the sofa.

I read it for a few minutes. How strange it was to read old news. There was one story that interested me. A woman's body, or part of it, had been found in the River Deben near Woodbridge. She had been dead for a few weeks. The story said that she had a lover and the police were looking for him. I knew where that river was. I'd been there with Linda after shopping in Woodbridge once. We had gone down to look at the boats. In my mind I could see the body of that poor woman lying in the river.

I stopped thinking about the story. It was making me feel unhappy. I looked at the date on the newspaper. It was yesterday's. That was odd. Perhaps Linda had asked someone to look after the house? That would explain why someone had parked a car next to the house, too. I would ask her, I thought, and then decided it was time to go to the pub and wait for her to phone.

I put on my jacket and drove to the only pub in Little Moreton. The *Ancient Mariner* pub was an ugly building standing by itself at one end of the village. It wasn't good weather. It was cold and there was a strong east wind. I drove slowly and, as I got closer to the pub, it started to rain.

I went inside and saw a fire and people talking and laughing. I felt better immediately. For some reason the house and the bad weather made me feel strange. I went to the bar and asked the woman for a small whisky with water.

'You're not from round here, are you?' She smiled and gave me my whisky.

'Yes. Well, I've been here before. My wife and I bought a house here some time ago. She comes down here a lot. In fact she's going to phone me here tonight. She's coming down by train and I'm going to pick her up.'

'I see. Well, she hasn't phoned yet. Which house did you say?' She seemed interested.

'It's on the main road. On the left as you come into the village,' I explained.

'Oh, you mean the Parker's old place? Of course. Does your wife have fair hair?'

'Yes she does. Long fair hair. You've probably seen her.'

'Yes, I think have. She doesn't come in here, though. I'm Mary Banks. This is my pub.'

'How do you do? I'm Carl Anderson.'

'I'll let you know when she phones. Now, are you hungry?' She gave me the menu and I sat at the bar to be near the phone.

I had dinner and a few drinks. Not many. I was driving. I sat waiting by the phone all night but Linda didn't ring. Once, when it was nearly eleven, the phone rang. I jumped up to answer it, but it was a man's voice asking for Mary. I gave her the phone.

I could hear Mary getting quite angry.

'No, he's not here,' she was saying. 'He hasn't been in all night. And I haven't seen your taxi. You should look after that brother of yours.'

She called out to the people in the pub: 'Anyone seen mad Tom tonight?' Nobody had seen him and she said this to the man on the phone.

Five minutes later though, a man came into the pub and began asking if anyone wanted a taxi to the station. He was a large man with a lot of black hair that fell over his eyes. He was rather dirty with what looked like dried blood on his face. When he came in most people stopped talking, but nobody said they wanted a taxi. Mary went up to him and spoke to him quietly.

'Your brother's looking for you. He wants his taxi back. You know you shouldn't be driving that car.'

The man said nothing, then turned round and left. The pub remained quiet for a minute or two until a man on my right said, 'I see Bill's letting his mad brother play taxis again.'

'It's not right, Tom driving a taxi,' said Mary. 'People are not safe with a man like that.' Then she stopped. She had seen the look on my face. 'What's the matter, Mr Anderson?'

'Nothing. It's nothing,' I replied. But in my head I saw Linda standing on the platform and mad Tom waiting in his taxi outside.

Chapter 3 *Mad Tom*

I left the pub quickly. I didn't like this talk about mad people. Maybe it was the newspaper article I had seen that afternoon, but I began to worry for Linda. Where was she? Was she safe? I had to go to the train station and wait for Linda. The weather was still not very good and I drove slowly in the dark – there were no street lights and not many houses. After a few minutes I saw the lights of a car behind me and turned round. The car passed me and I thought I saw the words PARKER'S TAXI on its side. For some reason I felt cold with fear. I decided to go home first to see if Linda was there. Maybe she'd forgotten to call me and had come straight there. I saw the lights of our house were on. I thought it must be Linda.

I ran up to the front door and opened it. Every light in the house was on. I called out 'Linda, Linda are you there?' There was no answer, but as I ran through the sitting-room and into the kitchen I heard a car start outside. I looked into the blackness outside and saw the back lights of a car going away down the road. I was sure it was the taxi that had passed me earlier. It must have been parked on the opposite side of the road but I hadn't seen it. What did that man want with me, with my house? All I could think about was that madman's face as he drove towards the station and my Linda.

I ran out of the house and got into the car again and

drove as fast as I could along the narrow country roads towards the station. It wasn't easy driving as I didn't know the road well – I was breathing fast.

At last I saw the lights of Woodbridge. I followed the signs to the station. I drove through the centre of the town and down to the river. I parked in the small car park outside the station and looked around. I couldn't see a taxi anywhere. In fact there were no other cars in the car park. About five or six people were coming down the steps from the station.

'Was that the last train from London?' I asked an old man.

'Yes. There are no more trains tonight, I'm afraid. Where do you want to go?'

'Nowhere. It doesn't matter,' I said. I looked up and down the station and waited for five minutes or so. There was no sign of Linda. She'd missed the train or had decided not to come after all.

Was she still angry with me and had decided to make me wait? There was nothing I could do about that. I phoned the flat in London from a public phone near the station but there was nobody there. Then I phoned Melissa. Her answerphone was on and I left a message for Linda to ring me at the pub.

Linda must still be at the party, I told myself. She's enjoying herself and just forgot the time. She probably remembered and called the pub after I'd left. I decided to go back to the pub and ask. I didn't want to think that something might have happened to her, nor did I want to think about mad Tom.

I had a sudden need to talk to someone about my fears. I

thought of Mary who had been friendly to me in the pub. Yes, she would understand, I thought. She would stop the terrible thoughts that were beginning to fill my head. I drove slowly back through the town and took the lonely country road to Little Moreton. There was no other traffic on the road. I passed our house on the left as I entered the village. The lights were still on but I didn't stop. When I reached the *Ancient Mariner* it was in darkness. I looked at my watch. Twelve-thirty. It was long after closing time and Mary was probably fast asleep. I got out of the car and walked towards the pub. I heard a voice in the darkness.

'Who's there?' It was Mary. She was speaking from an upstairs window.

'I'm sorry. I know it's late but I want to know if my wife's called yet.'

'No,' said Mary, 'she hasn't phoned. I think it's very late to call now, don't you?' I nodded my head. I didn't know what to do now. I just stood there outside the pub in the rain and nodded. Then I said, 'Could I talk to you about that man in the taxi? I know this sounds stupid . . .'

She didn't wait for me to finish. 'Wait a minute. I'll come down.'

A light went on somewhere in the pub and then I heard Mary unlock the door.

'Come in,' she said. I went inside and she told me to go and sit in her sitting-room, which was behind the bar.

'Are you sure my wife hasn't phoned?' I asked.

'I'm sorry, she hasn't. Are you very worried? Have you been to the train station?'

'Yes, and she wasn't there. Of course I'm worried. With that madman driving around in a taxi? You know when I left here Tom was waiting for me outside my house. I can't be sure, but I think he'd been inside the house. Anyway, he drove off quickly when I arrived. What do you think about that?' I sounded angry as well as afraid.

'Yes, well I might be able to explain that,' Mary said. 'You see Tom Parker – the man who came into the pub tonight and asked anyone if they wanted a taxi – well, he used to live in that house. In the house you bought. They had to move out when their father died. He and his brother, that is. His mother died when he was a baby. It made him go a bit strange. Then the father died and they had to leave the village. The father was drowned, you see. Tom was with him at sea in the fishing boat but he couldn't save his dad. Tom couldn't swim. He's always been frightened to get in the water.

'I'm sure he wouldn't hurt you or your wife, Mr Anderson. He just looks a bit strange and he frightens people if they don't know him, that's all,' Mary said.

'You're probably right,' I said. 'I just don't know what to think. If only Linda had rung to say she wasn't coming . . .'

'Oh, you know how it is if you're having a good time at a party,' Mary said. 'The last thing you want to do is find a phone and ring someone and tell them you don't want to leave.' Mary smiled at me in a warm way. What she said made sense and I thought that it would be better if I waited until the next day. I was sure everything would be all right and I suddenly felt very tired.

'Look. Why don't you stay here tonight? You can sleep on the sofa and I'll bring you some blankets.'

I agreed. I didn't want to go back to the house. Perhaps I would feel better in the morning, I thought to myself.

Mary left me on the sofa and went back upstairs. I fell asleep almost immediately, but I slept badly. I woke several times after terrible dreams. I was running after Linda on the beach. I could just see her in front of me. Her fair hair and long slim legs were so near I could almost touch them. But she was running into the sea and I couldn't stop her. She was drowning and there was mad Tom shouting at me: 'Let her go, let her go . . . !'

Chapter 4 *A voice in the dark*

It was seven when I woke the next morning, and still dark. I knew I couldn't sleep any more and I felt uncomfortable on the small sofa. There was no noise from upstairs. Mary was still asleep. It was too early to phone Linda in London. She would be angry if I woke her up at this time. I decided to get up and go for a walk on the beach. I left the pub as quietly as I could.

There was a strong wind from the sea and I could hear the waves on the stones. At least it wasn't raining. I walked behind the pub and across the car park, through some long grass and then down to the sea. About a hundred metres along I saw a car parked on the beach. There was no road and I couldn't see how it had got there. It was a strange place to leave a car.

When I got closer I saw that it was an old car and the tyres were flat. It had probably not been driven for some time. I looked up and down the beach but there was nobody around. I looked through the dirty windows. There were some man's clothes on the front seat: a shirt and some trousers and one black shoe. Had someone spent the night there? That one shoe was strange. Perhaps the other one was under the seat? I tried to open the driver's door but it was locked.

In the distance I could just see the church. I started to walk towards it. It was over a kilometre but I walked quickly and reached it in less than fifteen minutes. I like churches and last time Linda and I had walked this way I'd wanted to go and have a look inside. Linda said it was boring so we didn't. In fact, the last time I'd been inside a church with Linda was when we got married.

I didn't expect to find the church open at this time on a Saturday morning, but it was. I pushed open the heavy wooden door and went inside. It was dark but there was enough light for me to see a large picture on a wall. I could just see a large whale with a man in its mouth. It must be the story of Jonah and the whale, I thought. I couldn't remember ever seeing a picture like that in a church before. Then I heard the church door open and I jumped. A voice in the darkness said:

'You don't usually see a painting like that in a house of God, do you?' It wasn't the first time I had heard that voice.

'No, no. Is it Jonah and the whale . . . ?' I asked. I thought perhaps I shouldn't be in the church so I went on: 'I'm sorry, you see the door was open and I thought I . . .'

The man continued. 'Maybe it is and maybe it isn't. All I know is that you never know what might happen at sea.' I looked at the picture again, the large body of the whale and the small, white body of the man in the mouth of the animal. Then I heard the door at the back of the church close. The man had gone. I tried to remember where I had heard his voice before.

I didn't want to stay in the church any longer. I hurried outside and down to the beach. There was no sign of the man. It was still quite dark, but it was nearly seven thirty and the sky was beginning to change colour. I thought it was late enough now to call Linda again.

It was still difficult to see on the beach, but as I walked near the sea I saw something in the water. It was being pulled backwards and forwards by the waves. I bent down to pick it up. It was a woman's shoe. I don't know why but I immediately thought of the newspaper story about the woman's body that had been found in the River Deben. It was a small yellow shoe with a low heel, just like the sort of shoes that Linda wore. At that moment I saw the other shoe. It was higher up on the beach and was completely dry. It hadn't been in the sea. What worried me was that the shoes weren't old. Someone had thrown them away. In fact the shoes were almost new. Whose shoes were they?

I walked and then ran back to the *Ancient Mariner* carrying the shoes. The door was open and Mary was washing glasses.

'Morning, Mr Anderson,' she said. 'You're up early. Did you sleep all right?' She saw the shoes I was carrying. 'What have you got there?'

I put the shoes on the bar. 'I found them on the beach. How do you think they got there?' Mary put down the glass she was drying and picked up one of the shoes.

'Well, anyone could have . . .' and then she looked up at me. 'You don't think they belong to your wife, do you?'

'I don't know. I don't think it's possible. She's still in London.' I wanted Mary to tell me I was right. Of course they couldn't be Linda's shoes, I told myself.

But then Mary told me something that worried me even more.

'Look, Mr Anderson, this is probably nothing

important, but the postman came this morning and I told him about you staying here last night. I told him you bought the Parker's house and he said he's seen your wife now and then.'

'Well, of course he has. She often comes here for the weekend.'

'Yes, well, there's more. The postman said he saw your wife in town, in Woodbridge, yesterday evening. She was with someone, he thinks. Of course, he could be wrong.'

'Oh, my God. I knew it. Something is very wrong. She could be dead by now. She could have lost these shoes when . . .' I didn't want to think about it. I looked inside one of the shoes. Yes, they were a size four. Linda's size. They must be hers.

'Mary,' I said, 'call the police. I'm going back to the beach.' I ran out of the pub and down to the beach again. I ran towards the church and as close to the sea as possible. I tried to remember exactly where I'd found the shoes.

Then in the distance I saw something lying on the beach. It was about two metres from the sea and it looked like a body. I ran as fast as I could and, as I ran, I could hear myself repeating, 'Oh no, no, no. Please Linda. You must be OK!'

As I reached the thing I saw it was grey and covered with blood. I fell down beside it. I didn't want to look. There was a strong smell of fish. I looked. It *was* a fish. An enormous fish. I was crying now and saying to myself, 'Thank God, thank God it's not you, Linda.' I stood up and then I saw that the fish had no head. It looked as if someone had cut it off with a knife. I felt sick. Then I saw a man's shoe. It had blood on it, and it was the same as the shoe in the car on the beach. I ran back to the pub.

Mary was putting the phone down as I came into the bar.

'Mary, whose car is it on the beach? There's a shoe in it the same as the one with blood on it.'

I was speaking so quickly that Mary didn't understand what I was saying. She told me to slow down and explain.

'What shoe are you talking about? That car belongs to Tom Parker. He doesn't drive it, but he lives in it sometimes. I told you he was a bit strange. He likes to be near the sea.'

'Well, there's a fish down there on the beach. I thought it was my wife, at first. And its head's been cut off and there's a shoe under it. There's a shoe like that in the old car. Have you called the police?' I stopped for a second and Mary took my arm and sat me down.

'Now Mr Anderson. You've found a fish without its head and a couple of shoes that probably belong to poor Tom. Now that doesn't mean something has happened to your wife, does it?' Mary spoke in a soft, calm voice.

'Why don't you phone her in London and find out where she really is? I'll get you a cup of coffee.'

I phoned the flat but there was nobody there. I phoned Melissa, too, and her answerphone was still on. When Mary came back with my coffee I tried to sound normal.

'Mary, I think something *has* happened to my wife. She isn't in London as far as I know and you say she has been seen in Woodbridge. With this madman living in a car on the beach and driving taxis and killing fish I feel I must do something. Do you understand?'

She could see I was getting worried again. 'Why don't

you go back to your house? I'll phone PC Grant. He's the policeman in Great Moreton. We don't have a policeman in Little Moreton. I'll tell him where you are and he can go and find you there.'

I had to agree to that and so I drove back to the house.

Chapter 5 *The smell of death*

Driving back to the house I began to think and hope that Linda was waiting for me. I could see the house when I turned into the road. The lights must still be on but now that it was daytime I couldn't tell. I could see the empty space where I usually parked my car. I felt pleased that nobody else was there.

When I opened the door I called out Linda's name. She wasn't there, but there was a terrible smell. I thought the food that Linda had left in the fridge must be bad. I put it all into plastic bags and threw it outside. I poured the rest of the milk down the sink. Then I opened all the downstairs windows. The smell was less but it was still there.

The village policeman arrived a few minutes later. I was pleased to see him.

'Come in. You must be PC Grant. I can't give you a cup of coffee, I'm afraid. Unless you take it black. The milk's gone bad.' He looked at me and smiled.

'That's all right, I've just had one. I thought I could smell something.'

'Oh dear. I'll have to clean the fridge,' I said. PC Grant sat down on the sofa and I sat on a chair. There was a photograph of Linda and me on a small table beside the sofa. It was taken soon after we were married. We both looked so happy. Now it made me want to cry.

But I wasn't going to do that in front of a policeman. He picked the photograph up.

'So this is Mrs Anderson?' PC Grant said.

'Yes. It was taken about five years ago. She's very beautiful, isn't she?'

'Yes, sir. She's a very pretty woman. Now what makes you think she may be in some kind of trouble?'

I told him everything that had happened and I showed him the shoes. The shoe that had been in the sea was dry now, but it looked darker than the other one. He seemed quite interested in the shoes.

'This one smells a bit like fish. It's been in the sea, you say?' He put the shoes down again. 'And you say they are your wife's shoes?'

'They could be,' I said. 'They're her size. She takes a size four shoe. That's quite small.'

'And you're sure these are Mrs Anderson's shoes?' the policeman asked.

'Um, no, but she wears shoes like this,' I said. I could see he was losing interest.

'Well, Mr Anderson. You say your wife was going to a party in London last night and you've phoned her and she's not at home. I think she may be on her way then, don't you?' He smiled kindly at me.

'And as for young Tom Parker. I've known him for a long time. He may not live like the rest of us but I'm sure he wouldn't hurt anybody. He lost his father, you know. He thinks his father will come back if he waits long enough. Very sad.' PC Grant stood up to leave.

'I know about that,' I said, 'but I'm sure he's been in this house. Last night he was outside in his car when I got back from the pub. And all the lights were on inside the house.' I hoped this would make him do something.

'Ah, now that's not right,' said the policeman. 'It was Tom's house a few years back, but he mustn't do things like that. I'll speak to him. Make sure you keep the house locked, sir. All right? Now I must go.' He walked to the door. 'I'll take this photograph of your wife, if that's all right with you.'

I agreed and he put the photograph in his pocket. I knew it was no good trying to make him understand. I watched PC Grant get on his bicycle and go down the road.

I sat down and thought about what I could do. I could phone Linda's parents and see if they knew anything. If Linda had decided to do something different, go away with Melissa, they would probably know. I didn't want to call them, however, because then they would know there was a problem between Linda and me. Perhaps the policeman was right and Linda was on her way here.

I could go to the station again and phone Melissa from there, I thought. If she wasn't there I'd then call her parents. I decided to do that, but first I needed a bath and clean clothes – I had been wearing the same clothes since leaving London.

I went into the kitchen and cleaned the fridge and the floor. The floor was very dirty. That wasn't like Linda. She hated dirt. I went upstairs to start the bath. The smell seemed stronger upstairs. I went in the bathroom and turned on the taps. I looked in the mirror. I looked tired. The smell was stronger than ever. I opened the bathroom window.

Then I went into our bedroom. The terrible smell of death hit me in the face. I looked at the bed. The blankets were pulled up over the pillow. There was blood on the blankets. There was somebody in the bed! It didn't move or even breathe. It must be dead, I thought. I felt my heart beating hard. I couldn't breathe properly. For a few moments I stood by the door. I could not move. I was very scared. Then, slowly, I walked over to the bed. I knew I had to pull back the blankets and look at what was there.

In my head I saw the beautiful, white body of my wife lying there. Her eyes were open and there was a sad, sweet smile on her lips. But she was dead. She'd left me and I would never know why . . .

I had to do it. I had to look. I pulled back the blankets quickly with my eyes closed. The smell was terrible. I opened them and looked down. For a second I thought I was looking at the bloody body of my wife. Then I saw it was the grey and bloody head of a very big fish. I felt sick and happy at the same time. Then I started to cry. The whole thing was too much for me. I threw the blankets over the fish head and ran down the stairs. I ran into the garden and was sick.

'This isn't real,' I thought. I was going mad. I was shaking and crying, but I got in my car and drove to the pub. The door of the pub was open and Mary came out. I got out of the car and walked towards her.

'What is it? What's wrong?' she asked. She got to me as I fell to the ground. The next thing I knew some men were carrying me into the pub. They laid me down on the sofa. Mary was standing looking at me and telling the men to call a doctor. She looked very worried.

'No,' I said, 'Don't call a doctor. There's something in my bed. Someone has put a fish head in my bed. I thought it was Linda!' I put my head in my hands. 'How could they, how could they?' My whole body was shaking and I began to laugh and cry at the same time. What a terrible, terrible joke! I thought.

Mary went over to the phone. I heard her calling for a doctor. Then she phoned the police.

Chapter 6 *Dead father*

I was still lying on the sofa when the doctor arrived. He looked at me and asked me a few questions. Then he put his hand on my shoulder. I felt like a child.

'Now, Mr Anderson, you must rest. You're very tired and you need to sleep. I'll ask Mary to get you something to drink. I'll give you some pills. You'll feel better soon. Mary will take care of you.' He went over to talk to Mary and they went outside. After he had gone she brought me a drink and sat down by the sofa.

'How are you feeling, Mr Anderson?' she asked.

'Please, you can call me Carl. I don't feel very good, but I don't think I'm mad. The doctor thinks I'm mad, doesn't he? Well, what do you think, Mary?' I said.

'I don't think you're mad, Carl,' she said, 'but you are very worried about your wife. That makes you think everybody is against you.' She smiled at me kindly.

'Yes, yes, of course I'm worried. My wife has disappeared. Then you tell me someone has seen her. Then there is this madman, and the next thing I find half a dead fish on the beach and its head in my bed! How would you feel . . . ?' I was angry and speaking loudly.

'Sssshhhh,' said Mary. 'Calm down.'

I needed to talk, to find an explanation to what was happening, but I spoke more softly. 'I'm sure that Tom put it there, but I don't understand why. It's a very bad joke.

He must hate me.'

Mary shook her head. 'No, I don't think he hates you,' she said. 'I don't think it has anything to do with you or your wife. Anyway, the police are looking for him now. I told them what happened. They're coming here later to talk to you about it. But now you must try and sleep. The doctor has given me some pills. If you take one of these it will help you to sleep.' She held out a small white pill and a glass of water. I didn't want to take it but my head hurt and I knew that I needed to sleep.

When I woke up it was light. I heard voices in the room. It was PC Grant and Mary. I could hear other voices too, so I knew that the pub was open. Mary walked towards the door.

'How are you feeling, Carl?'

'Fine,' I said. 'I think.' My head hurt a bit.

'I'll have to go back in the bar,' said Mary. 'We're busy at the moment. You two can have a talk.' She shut the door to the sitting room and the policeman sat down on a chair opposite me.

'I have come to tell you that we've picked up Tom Parker. He's at the police station now. He's the one who put the fish in your bed. He's told us all about it. Actually, sir, he doesn't think it's a fish. He thinks it's his father. His father died at sea . . . He also said something about his girlfriend coming back from the sea. Well, he found the fish on the beach. He thought it was his father and so he took it home to bed. That's what he told us. It's sad, isn't it?'

'His father? Now I know the man is completely mad,' I said. 'But why does he think it's his father?

'Well, Tom Parker has always been a bit strange. He thinks that people who die in the sea will come back to life. Something like that. He told us his father had come back to him so he put him to bed . . .'

This is mad, I thought. This policeman is telling me things that don't seem real. I just wanted to know where Linda was.

'What's Tom done with my wife?' I said to PC Grant. 'You know she was seen in Woodbridge on Friday. She was with someone. Perhaps Tom picked her up from the station and took her somewhere and . . .' I was getting angry again.

PC Grant stood up to leave. I think he thought I was madder than Tom.

'I don't know what's happened to your wife, sir, but Tom doesn't know anything about your wife.'

'Did you show Tom my wife's photograph? What did he say?'

'No, sir,' he replied. 'I put the photograph on the wall in the station. That way if anyone has seen her they'll tell us. Now, it's not right that Tom went into your house and he won't do that again. We took some keys off him. We'd like to see if they're the keys to the house.'

'He has a key to my house?' I asked, surprised. I took my keys out of my pocket and gave him one of them. PC Grant took the key and left the room. He returned a minute later.

'Yes,' he said. 'It's the same key.'

'How did he get a key?'

'We don't know, sir. Is it OK if I go to your house and take a look round?'

'Yes,' I said, 'OK, but I am coming with you. I just want to make some phone calls first.' I stood up from the sofa and then sat down again immediately. I didn't feel quite right.

'I don't think that's a good idea,' said PC Grant. 'You make your phone calls and I'll see what I can do about this fish head. You need to relax. I think you'll probably find Mrs Anderson safe at home.' When PC Grant had gone Mary came back into the room.

'PC Grant has told me about Tom,' she said. 'Try not to worry. I'm making some lunch for us. Then we can go to your house. I'll help you clean up the bedroom if you want.'

'That's very kind,' I said. 'But I want to make a few phone calls first. I'm going to call the flat. If no-one's there I'll call Melissa. She was with Linda on Friday . . . I might call Linda's parents as well. They may know something. What do you think?' I was so worried and tired that I was finding it hard to decide things by myself.

'Good idea, Carl. Use the phone in here.' She went to the kitchen and left me alone to make my phone calls. I phoned the flat first. There was no-one there or at Melissa's place. I then called Linda's parents. Her mother answered. She was surprised to hear my voice. I didn't often phone them.

'Carl! How nice to hear from you. How are you?' She obviously didn't know anything. I didn't want to tell her too much.

'Hi there, Joan. I'm at the house in Little Moreton. I'm waiting for Linda to arrive. She was at a party last night. Did you speak to her yesterday? I've phoned the flat but there's no-one there.' I hoped I didn't sound worried.

'I spoke to her on Wednesday, I think. I'm sorry things aren't very good between you. If there's anything that I can do.' I wasn't pleased that Linda had told her mother about our problems.

'Well, everything's all right now. We're spending the weekend together down here in Little Moreton. I just wanted to know what train she's catching. In fact I'd better go to the station now. Bye, Joan.' I wanted to get off the phone as quickly as possible.

'Oh, I'm glad everything's all right. Have a good weekend,' she said. I didn't think she sounded very sure and I wished I hadn't called her.

Mary came in with some food, but I couldn't eat anything.

'I can't understand why Linda told her mother that she wasn't very happy, but hadn't told me before.' Then I remembered something the policeman had said.

'Mary, who was Tom's girlfriend? What happened to her?'

'She was called Jenny. She wasn't really his girlfriend. She was in love with his brother, Bill. Unfortunately Bill wasn't interested. She used to go round with Tom so that she could be near Bill. Then one day a few weeks ago she disappeared. They found her body in the river a few days ago.'

'Oh yes.' I had remembered the story in the newspaper. 'They found her body in the river, didn't they? And her head had been cut off.' I was thinking about the fish head in my bed.

'Well, that's what the newspapers say, but we don't know. Anyway, Tom had nothing to do with it. He was with his brother at the time. They were in London, I think.'

Mary didn't seem to want to talk about it any more.

'Come on then,' she said. 'Let's go and clean up this bedroom.'

We went in Mary's car. She didn't think I should drive. When we got to the house she told me to stay in the car for a minute.

'I'll go and see what it looks like first.' I let her. I did not really want to smell that terrible smell or see that fish again. I looked at the house. I was beginning to hate that house. She came out after a few minutes carrying some blankets.

'It's not too bad. The police must have taken the fish head away. I'll take these blankets and wash them at the pub. Oh . . .' she put her hand in her pocket. 'There's a letter for you.'

She handed me the letter through the car window and I looked at it. I saw my name in Linda's writing. My hands were shaking as I opened it.

Dear Carl
I'm sorry but it's finished between us. Please don't try to find me. I am all right.
Be happy.

love

Linda

I looked at the letter without saying anything for a minute or two. I couldn't believe it. Mary had opened the back of the car to put the blankets in. She saw me put my head in my hands.

'Carl, what's the matter? Who is the letter from?' Without a word I handed her the letter. She read it.

'Oh dear. Carl, I am so sorry.'

I still had the envelope in my hands. I looked at the stamp. I wasn't thinking right, but for some reason I saw something strange on the envelope.

'Mary, this can't be right. Look.' I showed her the envelope. 'This was posted in Woodbridge . . . Why was she in Woodbridge if she was going to leave me?' I suddenly thought that this letter wasn't true.

'Someone has made her write this letter,' I said. 'I'm sure that Tom has done something to her. Look what he did to that girl and the fish. Now he's got Linda and he won't let her go. She's probably somewhere near here. She may be dead, like Jenny. Oh dear, my poor Linda. What am I going to do?' Mary looked at me as if I was mad. But I thought I was right. I thought I knew the answers.

Chapter 7 *She still loves me*

Mary and I went back to the police station and I showed them the letter. They just looked at me sadly.

'It's difficult when your wife leaves you,' one of the policemen said.

I tried to tell them that I didn't think it was true, that this madman had taken her somewhere. But they didn't believe me. They said that Tom wouldn't do something like that. They just told me to go home.

I drove back to London that evening. I wasn't going to stay in that house by the sea a moment longer. Mary was very kind. She said she would ring if she heard anything. I decided I was going to try and see Melissa. She was Linda's friend and she had to help me find her. She'd understand why I was worried, I thought.

As I drove the car fast along the country roads towards London I thought about all the things that had happened. I couldn't believe that Linda had left me. I knew we had some difficult times, and sometimes she didn't like me to spend so much time at the office. But that was because she wanted to be with me. She loved me. Then I tried to remember the last time she'd said she loved me . . .

The first thing I did when I got back to the flat was to phone Melissa. I wanted her to come with me and speak to the police, to tell them Linda wouldn't leave me.

'Melissa, is that you? It's Carl here.'

'What is it, Carl?' She didn't want to speak to me.

'It's about Linda. You must believe me. Something has happened to her,' I said quickly.

'What are you talking about, Carl? How do you know? She was all right on Friday,' she answered.

'Of course she was all right on Friday. She went to that party with you, didn't she?' Melissa didn't say anything, so I went on. 'She was coming down to our house in Little Moreton after the party, but she didn't arrive. I thought she had missed the train or something. Didn't you get my message?' I asked.

'Yes, Carl. I got your message, but she wasn't with me.' Melissa didn't sound worried at all. Didn't anyone understand that my wife had disappeared and was probably with some madman who might hurt her?

'For God's sake, Melissa. There's this man in Little Moreton who is completely mad. He lives in an old car on the beach and he put this fish head in my bed. He's got Linda. I'm sure he has.' I thought that Melissa would understand how serious it was, but I thought I heard her laughing.

'Carl, really!' she said. 'Are you mad? You know Linda was unhappy with you. That's why she was staying with me. You were in love with *work*. Not with *her*. You left her alone too much. She was very unhappy. I don't know anything else, but I'm sure you don't need to worry about her. Look, I'm busy, I have to go.' She put the phone down.

I was angry that Melissa didn't think it was serious. Also she had no idea how much Linda and I loved each other. She was wrong about everything.

I went into the kitchen of our flat to make myself a cup

of coffee. There were two dirty cups in the sink. I was sure I had not left them there. Had Linda come back to the flat after the party? I went into the bedroom and opened the wardrobe. Linda had taken most of her clothes to Melissa's house the week before, but she'd left a yellow dress in there. It was a party dress. I remembered the yellow shoes I'd found on the beach.

I was now sure that she had come back to the flat during the weekend. I went back into the kitchen and looked at the cups. One of the cups had lipstick on it. The other cup had sugar in it. Linda didn't take sugar in her coffee. I didn't understand what was going on. If Linda had come back to the flat after the party, why hadn't she phoned me? As I sat down at the table with my coffee the phone rang. It was Mary.

'What is it? Have they found Linda? Is she all right?' My questions came so fast that I didn't wait for Mary to answer them.

'Slow down, Carl, slow down. Nothing like that. I thought you wanted to know if there was any news. It's just that . . .'

'I'm sorry, Mary. Things are so difficult for me. You know Linda's friend, Melissa, she won't tell me anything. She thinks it's a big joke and says I should stop worrying. Anyway, what is it? What have you heard?'

'Nothing,' she said. 'I just wanted to see if you were all right.'

'I'm OK,' I said. I didn't want to tell her about the coffee cups I had found.

'Carl, I just think the police are right. I don't think Tom has anything to do with your wife.'

'Well, I don't agree,' I said. 'I think he's done something to her.'

Mary could hear my anger. She was silent at the other end of the phone. 'And what's this village policeman going to do about it?' I went on, shouting at her now. 'He cut the head off that fish. And how did he get a key to the house?'

'I don't know,' Mary said, 'though the house used to belong to his family. Maybe he has an old key?'

'Well, it's not his house now. It's mine. Mine and Linda's. The man is mad. They should put him in prison.'

Mary was silent again. I realised it was wrong to be angry at Mary.

'I'm sorry, Mary. You've been very kind to me. I don't know *what* to think anymore . . .'

'That's OK,' Mary said.

'Listen, if you hear anything about Linda will you ring me, please? I have to work tomorrow, but . . .' I gave Mary my phone number at work, thanked her again for being so kind and put the phone down.

I went to work that week, but it was very difficult. I didn't tell anybody there about what had happened. I knew they wouldn't understand, but I couldn't concentrate on work and I didn't sleep very well. Every time the phone rang I thought it would be Linda, but it wasn't . . . she didn't ring.

Mary didn't ring either. On Thursday it was the Great Moreton police who rang me. I was at work and it was difficult to talk.

'Mr Anderson, it's PC Grant from Great Moreton police station. We have discovered a body on the beach . . .' As soon as I heard those words I stopped listening. I could see the body of my wife on the stones of the beach. The cold sea was washing over her legs. She was wearing a yellow dress and yellow shoes. She was dead but still very beautiful . . . My life was over.

' . . . he's been in the sea a couple of days. I am afraid we do need to speak to you as soon as possible.' I heard the word 'he's' and almost shouted down the phone.

'It's a *man's* body, is it?' I was so happy. I nearly laughed until I saw people in the office were looking at me.

'Yes, sir. I said it was the body of Tom Parker. We would like you to come down to Great Moreton as soon as possible to talk to us. We need to know where you have been for the last few days and so on.' PC Grant spoke slowly and politely. I knew this was serious.

'Where do you think I've been? I've been at work. I'm at work now. How did you get my number?' My voice was getting louder. People in the office had started to look interested.

I wanted to stop this conversation. 'I'll come down as soon as possible. Is there any other news?'

'No, sir. Are you asking about Mrs Anderson? I thought she would be back home by now . . .'

'Well, she isn't.' If we'd been in the same room I would have hit PC Grant. 'And I want to know what you are doing about it.'

'Sorry to hear that. We could talk about your wife as well. I'll expect you soon, then?'

Suddenly I felt as if I'd done something wrong. What did the policeman mean by 'we could talk about my wife as well'? Did he think I'd killed Tom Parker? Did he think I'd killed my wife, too?

I told my boss I had to take two days holiday. I said there was a problem with the house. I couldn't give him the real reason. He wasn't very happy about it.

I went back to the flat and put some clean clothes in a bag. I saw the yellow dress again and put it into the bag with my clothes. I don't know why exactly. I thought maybe Linda might need it. Then I got in the car and drove to Little Moreton.

Chapter 8 *Too many questions*

I arrived in Little Moreton in the early evening. I didn't want to go to the police immediately, and I didn't want to go the house on my own, so I went to the *Ancient Mariner.* I walked into the pub and saw that Mary was busy behind the bar. I sat down at a table. After a few minutes she came over. She could see from my face that something was wrong.

'What is it, Carl? Have you heard about Tom? I only heard this morning. The police say he'd been dead for two days.'

'Oh yes, they told me that. But did they tell you they think I killed him? Did they tell you they think I killed my wife?' Mary sat down.

'No, Carl, that can't be right. You must have made a mistake. It's not possible.' I got hold of her arm.

'Mary, you've got to help me. They want me to go and talk to them about Tom. Perhaps they think I was angry with him because I think he took my wife. I told them Linda hadn't come back. Now they may think I've killed her, too, because of Tom. Oh Mary, what am I going to do?'

'I'll come with you to the police. I'm sure they don't think that at all. It's no surprise to anyone that Tom has killed himself. It must be because of that fish and thinking it was his dad. Believe me, I thought it was going to happen one day,' said Mary. She got me a whisky and then told me to go and wait in the car.

Although I was still worried, Mary's words made me feel better. If only Linda would come back everything would be all right again. I hoped that Mary was right.

We drove to the police station in Great Moreton without saying much. It was the next village, about six kilometres from Little Moreton, and twice as large. We parked outside the station and I followed Mary inside. As we went in a tall, dark man was coming out. Mary said hello to him.

'You know everyone round here, do you?' I asked her.

'No, but that was Tom Parker's brother, Bill. He lives in Great Moreton somewhere. It's a good thing he's gone. He's a difficult man. Nobody likes him much.' I turned to look at the man but he'd gone. I think I saw a taxi driving away. Later I wished I'd looked at him more carefully.

PC Grant was waiting for us. Mary had phoned from the pub to say we were coming. He took me into a small room. There was another policeman in there already. Mary had to wait outside.

'Sit down, Mr Anderson. Thank you for coming to the station. I have a few questions to ask you.' Then both of them sat opposite me. There was a table between us. I put my arms on it. 'We want to know where you were from Monday to Wednesday? We also want to know when you last saw Mr Tom Parker?' PC Grant wasn't smiling and the other policeman looked very serious.

They asked lots of questions and I gave them the best answers I could. I was worried because I'd been alone for some of the time when I was in London. I was sure they were going to tell me they wanted me to stay, so I was surprised when PC Grant stood up.

'Thank you, Mr Anderson,' he said. 'That has been very useful. We're sorry about the problem with the fish. You know we spoke to Tom Parker about it. He was sure it was his father. When we told him it was just a fish he said he was going to look for his father again. We think he took his brother's boat and went out to sea. He couldn't swim, you know. Tom Parker was always afraid of the sea. It's not your fault, Mr Anderson.'

I got up and was about to leave when the other policeman said, 'Then there is the matter of your wife, Mr Anderson. We need to have a few words about that.' I sat down again and PC Grant looked at me.

'Mr Anderson, we know that you haven't seen your wife since last week. Is that right?'

'Yes,' I said.

'And that she had been staying with a friend and she was coming here on Friday night?'

'Yes,' I said.

'Then a postman in Great Moreton said that he saw your wife on Friday night in Woodbridge with a man. Are you sure that you didn't see your wife last weekend, Mr Anderson?'

I knew immediately what they were thinking. They thought I had got angry with Linda and had done something to her.

'No, I didn't see my wife last weekend,' I said. I was trying to stay calm. 'She may have been seen in Woodbridge, but that is only what the postman says. Yes,

I got a letter from her. It was posted in Woodbridge on Friday.'

'And in that letter she wrote you, sir,' the other policeman said, 'she said she was leaving you. Is that right?' I didn't like the way he spoke. It was as though he didn't believe anything I said. I was very confused at this moment – I didn't know what to think or do.

'She said she was leaving me,' I said, 'but I know that she was just angry with me . . . Are you married?' I asked PC Grant. 'If you are, then you'll know that sometimes it's difficult. Linda was staying with a friend for a few days. Then I phoned her and she agreed to come to our house in Little Moreton for the weekend. I was waiting for her and she didn't arrive. She was coming, but someone stopped her . . . I think she was on her way but something happened.' They had to believe me.

'Yes, Mr Anderson. That may all be true but can you explain why you went back to London if you thought your wife was here?' PC Grant was writing something down.

'Well, I needed to talk to one of her friends and I had to go back to work. I have an important job, you know.' This didn't sound so good now. I wished I hadn't gone back to work. Linda was right. I always thought my job was the most important thing.

I put my head in my hands. My life was in pieces. My wife had left me. A madman had come into the house, put a fish head in my bed, and then died. And now the police think I'd killed my wife because I was angry with her for leaving me. I was surprised when PC Grant put his hand on my arm and said in a kind way.

'All right, Mr Anderson. That's all for now. You can go. We would like you to stay in Little Moreton for the moment. We'll tell you if we have any news.' They both stood up and walked with me to the door. Mary was still waiting for me. She looked up and smiled.

'You've been a long time. Are you OK?'

'No, not really,' I answered. 'Let's get out of here.'

As we drove back to the pub I told Mary what the police had asked me. I said I thought they didn't believe everything I had said.

'But they let you go,' she said and I had to agree. 'What are you going to do now?' she asked.

'They said I must stay in Little Moreton for a few days. I'll go back to the house,' I answered.

'You can come back to the pub if you like.'

'No, thank you, Mary, but I want to go back to the house. It's my house and if Linda comes back I want to be there.'

We drove back and stopped outside the pub.

'Will you be all right? I don't like leaving you there at that house on your own. Are you sure you don't want to come back to the pub?' Mary asked.

'No, I'll be fine. I want to go to bed. I haven't been sleeping well and I'm tired. I'll sleep on the sofa. See you tomorrow.' She got out of the car and waved goodbye.

I drove on through the village to the house. It was dark and I was pleased to see that there were no lights on in the house and no taxi parked beside it. I got out of the car and locked it. I looked up and down the road. There was nobody and nothing to see. I decided at that moment to sell the house. I didn't like it any more. Perhaps I'd never liked it. I didn't like the countryside. It was too lonely out here. Linda would have to agree . . .

At this thought of Linda I suddenly felt sad and very tired. I opened the door and went inside and put out my hand to switch on the light. Nothing. The lights weren't working. At the same moment I thought I saw, standing in the doorway of the kitchen, a tall woman with long fair hair. And then she was gone.

'Who's there?' I shouted. Perhaps I was so tired I was seeing things that weren't there, I thought. And it was dark. Suddenly I felt more afraid than I ever had in my life. I heard another noise. Who was it? It couldn't be Tom. Tom was dead.

I shouted, 'Who's there. Who are you?' and ran into the kitchen in the dark, hitting things as I did. At first I couldn't see anything because it was so dark. I'll get a knife, or something, I thought. And I was just going to get one when I saw her . . .

Chapter 9 *Whose fault is it?*

The kitchen was not completely dark. There was some light coming through the window and I could just see the fridge and the sink. I was beginning to think I was going mad and needed to see a doctor, when something moved.

'Who is it? Come out so that I can see you!' I was almost screaming. Then I saw the tall woman come towards me through the darkness.

'Carl, it's me,' said a voice. It was Linda's voice. I wanted to believe it was Linda's voice. I put out my hand and touched her warm body. I fell down on my knees and put my arms around her. 'Oh my God, Linda. Is it you? Have you come back to me? Oh thank you, thank you. I knew you would. I knew it.' I was so happy.

'Yes, Carl, it's me,' she said. 'I want to talk to you. I shouldn't have . . .' I didn't give her time to finish.

'No, don't say anything,' I said. 'I'm so happy to have you back. I thought you were dead. I thought I would never see you again. Nothing else matters now . . .' I was crying. I couldn't move. I thought it was all over. Linda made me get off the floor.

'Let's go into the sitting-room. I turned off the lights, I'm sorry. I didn't want anybody to see me.' She walked slowly into the sitting-room and sat down on the sofa.

'I must tell you about it,' she began, but I didn't want her to speak.

'No, Linda. I don't want to know anything. I'm sorry I didn't spend more time on our marriage. I'm sorry about that, but you're back here with me now. That's the important thing. That's all I want.'

'Carl, I'm the one who is sorry,' she said. 'I can't come back. Everything is different now. Let me explain. Sit down, please.'

I sat down on the floor in front of her. I wanted to be as close to her as possible. I could smell her perfume and feel how warm her body was in the darkness. I felt warm and happy. Well, for a few seconds I felt warm and happy.

'You must listen to me, Carl.' Her voice was cold and distant. When she said my name like that I had to listen.

'I don't want to be your wife any more. I want to get a divorce. I came here to tell you that. I wanted to tell you before but I was afraid. I didn't want to hurt you, but I realise now there is no other way.

'After the office party I did catch the train . . . I was going to come here . . . I was going to come and tell you. But I couldn't do it. I didn't feel strong enough. I got off at Woodbridge. I wrote the letter to you then. That's when the postman saw me . . .

'Things had been very difficult between us for a long time, and then I met someone else. Now I love him and I'm going to stay with him. I'm sorry it has all been so terrible for you. It isn't fair, I know.'

The words hit me like stones. I couldn't see her face, it was too dark, and I put my hand towards her.

'No, Carl,' she said. 'Don't touch me. You mustn't touch me any more . . . Let me tell you how it happened.'

'Why, Linda? Why are you leaving me? I don't

understand. I can make everything better. I love you, you know I do. You must still love me.' I didn't want to hear her story, but she continued.

'I don't know if I still love you, Carl. I love someone else now. I've loved him for a long time and now I know I have to be with him and not you . . .' She stopped talking and looked out to the sea. I didn't say anything.

'It started when I found this house,' Linda said. 'This house by the sea. This house is very important to me . . . And I met him the first time I came here to Little Moreton, to this house. Of course, I didn't love him then. But he was kind and he was interested in me . . . You didn't have the time to come down here with me. Do you remember that, Carl?'

I did remember and I wished it wasn't true. I wished I had come down more often.

'Nothing happened for months, you know,' Linda went on. 'But every time I came here on my own he met me at the station and drove me here. He helped me to paint the house and buy the furniture . . . He didn't stay here with me but he often did things to the house when I went back to London. He stayed here when I wasn't here.'

'But Linda, why didn't you tell me about him? If I had known, perhaps . . .' I stopped because I wanted to cry again. I was very angry with myself.

'I don't know why I didn't tell you. I didn't love him then. But this house is my special place. I come here and I forget about my life in London.' She sounded sad.

'And forget about me,' I said.

'Yes . . . yes, I forget about you . . . I'm sorry.' She was beginning to cry.

'And why are you telling me now? Why did you say you were coming to see me here? You know it's been terrible for me. I thought I was going mad. This Tom, this madman who thought his dad was a fish. Do you know about that?' Then I had a terrible thought. 'Was it Tom Parker? Was he the man you loved?'

'No, no of course not. Poor old Tom. You know that Tom's family owned this house a long time ago, don't you? That's why he put the fish head in the bed. He thought he still lived here in this house and that was his father's bed. When he saw the fish he thought his father had come out of the sea and that if he put it in bed his father would return, he would get better. Poor Tom. He was quite mad. The fish must have smelt!' She laughed. I used to like to hear her laugh but now she seemed to be laughing at me. That didn't feel good.

'Don't laugh. It did smell and, you know, I thought it was your dead body. I didn't think it was funny. And the police think I killed him because I thought he had done something to you.'

'I'm sorry, Carl. No, it's not funny. Why did you think he wanted to hurt me?'

So I told her about seeing Tom for the first time. I told her what they said about him in the pub when I was waiting for her. I told her about going into the church and the yellow shoes in the sea. 'I thought I'd left them in London,' she said. 'Tom must have taken them.'

As I told her the story she said quietly to herself, 'Oh dear, oh no' over and over again.

'And now Tom's dead,' Linda said, 'and there's nothing we can do. That's my fault, too.'

'I don't understand,' I said again. 'What do you mean?'

'Tom was in love with a girl called Jenny,' Linda said. 'When she drowned a few weeks ago Tom was very unhappy. He spent a lot of time down on the beach looking out to sea. He slept in that car. Then he began to come to this house – his father's old house. When he saw me he suddenly thought that I was Jenny, his girlfriend, who had drowned . . . When I got off the train at Woodbridge last Friday, Tom saw me. He knew then I wasn't Jenny, but he took his brother's taxi and drove to Little Moreton to wait for Jenny at the house. That's when he saw you. He wasn't well. He probably thought for a minute you were his father. Then, when he saw the fish on the beach he wanted it to be his father. He was really mad in that last week. I hope he's happier now. He somehow knew his father wasn't coming back, so he went out to sea to find him. That's when he drowned . . . perhaps it was my fault.'

'Do the police know all of this?' I asked.

'No, not everything, but I wanted to tell you first. I wanted to explain. I'm going to tell the police now.'

'I'll come with you,' I said.

'No. I'll tell them by myself . . .' Linda got up and walked into the back garden. I followed her out. I was so surprised by it all I didn't say anything. Then I remembered the key.

'How did Tom get a key to the house?' I asked.

'He stole it from Bill.'

'Bill?'

'Bill Parker is the man I love. He's Tom's brother. I gave Bill a key to the house so he could do work on it while I was in London. Bill's been very kind to me. He's very sad about his brother.'

There were some stars in the sky which gave some light and I could see Linda looked very sad. I knew then, in that moment, that I was losing her.

'How long are you staying here for?' she asked.

'Why, does it matter?' I asked. I suddenly felt angry with her. 'Do you want to come and live here with that man?'

'Bill has done a lot of work on the house. It's his house, too. Of course I'll pay you for it.'

We walked around to the front of the house. 'I have to go, Carl,' she said. 'Bill's waiting for me down the road.'

I could see the lights of a car parked on the road about 100 metres away. It looked like a taxi. Slowly, I was beginning to understand.

'Goodbye, Carl.' She walked down the road towards the car and I stood alone by that house. I was trying to remember the face of the man who had passed Mary and me as we went into the police station a few hours ago. He was tall and dark, but I couldn't see his face.

I don't know how long I stood there. The car had long gone. I was shaking with cold. I went back in the house and up the stairs. I found myself sitting on the bed with Linda's yellow dress in my hands and I was crying. I sat there a long time and then I fell asleep.

In the morning I woke with the sun coming through the windows. I got out of bed and went to the bathroom. As I was washing my hands and face I looked in the mirror. I saw the face of an old man with sad eyes and hair that was starting to turn grey.

Chapter 10 *The yellow dress*

For a long time after Carl had finished his story I said nothing. We sat in the corner of the pub and drank our beer. It was nearly time for the pub to close. Carl looked out of the window. He seemed to be a long way away. I was thinking about what Carl had told me. I had some questions to ask but I didn't want to hurt Carl. He'd been hurt enough. In the end it was Carl who started speaking again.

'What are you thinking, John?' he asked. 'Are you thinking what a stupid man I was to let a woman like Linda go? Well, you're right, but what could I do? You know, I left that day and drove back to London. I didn't want to stay there. After what Linda told me I didn't feel it was my house any more. I've never been back to Little Moreton, to that house.'

I answered slowly. 'No, I don't think you are stupid to let Linda go. She'd decided that was what she was going to do. It was too late.' I hoped that I hadn't said too much to my friend. But Carl only heard what he wanted to hear.

'Yes, you're right. I should have seen what was happening a long time before. I shouldn't have let her buy that house. That place took her away from me. She said she didn't love this man at first, didn't she? It was the house and the countryside that she loved. And as for that mad Tom. Maybe if he hadn't died Linda would have come home with me. She thought it was her fault, you know. So she stayed because she felt sorry for his brother . . .'

I looked at Carl in surprise. Did Carl really believe this? But Carl went on: 'If only I had made her stay at home. That friend of hers, Melissa, she wasn't good for Linda. I'm sure she said bad things about me. I think she told Linda she should leave me. Linda still loves me. I know that. I will get her back in the end. You just wait and see.'

I wasn't sure what to say. Perhaps Carl didn't think it was his fault that Linda had left. Perhaps Carl didn't think it was anything to do with him. I was worried about my friend. I decided I had to say something to try and help Carl to understand what had happened.

'Carl, I'm very sorry that Linda's left you. But, you know, it sounds as if things had been wrong between you and Linda for a long time before she left you. Don't you think it would be a good idea to forget about her? You are still young. There are lots of other girls, aren't there?'

'John, you don't know what you're talking about. You don't know what happened. You don't understand about Linda and me. I told you my story because I thought you'd understand. Now all you can say is she's never coming back . . .' Carl looked out into space, thinking. I don't think he really believed what he was saying either.

'Yes, you're right,' he said after a few minutes. 'It's over. It's been over for a while, even though I still think about it a lot . . . Thanks, John,' he said.

'What for?' I asked.

'For listening to the story. It's helped me a lot. It's helped me to realise that I must move on, that I must start again. I didn't see the problems with Linda. I made mistakes. I didn't give her time. I worked too much . . . I don't work much these days. The company I worked for didn't want me. They thought I'd changed . . .'

We finished our beer. The pub was closing and we walked out into the night air together.

'Thanks again for listening,' Carl said.

'Don't mention it. Listen, call me, will you? Let's meet up again soon.' I gave him a card with my phone number on it. Then I watched him as he walked away. After he turned the corner the barman came out of the pub with a bag in his hand.

'Is this your bag?' he asked.

'No,' I said.

'Well, it was at the table where you were sitting,' the barman said and gave me the bag. I looked inside it. There was a yellow dress.

'It's my friend's bag,' I said to the barman. 'Thanks.' I ran down the road after Carl, but I couldn't see him anywhere. He'd gone.

I realised then that I had no idea where Carl lived and I didn't have his phone number. I looked in the bag again and pulled out the yellow dress. There was something else in there. At the bottom of the bag was a pair of small yellow shoes. One of the shoes was dirty.

I took the bag home that night. The next day I went back to the pub and gave my name and phone number to the barman.

'If my friend comes in looking for his bag, will you call me immediately?' I said.

But the barman never did ring and I haven't seen Carl since then. I thought perhaps that he might have gone mad like poor Tom. Then I realised that he might have left the bag in the pub on purpose. Perhaps Carl had been carrying the yellow dress and shoes around with him everywhere, but if he wanted to move on, to start a new life, he had to leave them behind. So I kept the bag with the yellow dress and shoes. Just in case.

Not long ago, I got married. We bought a house in the country. When I was packing my things I found the bag with the yellow dress and shoes. I hadn't seen Carl again but I hadn't forgotten his sad story. I didn't want to throw the bag away. Then one day my wife was cleaning the bedroom and she found the bag. I told her the story of Linda and Carl. When she asked me why I had kept the bag I thought for a moment and said;

'So that I never forget how easy it is to lose the things you love.' We both laughed, but we also knew there was some truth in it.